NEHEMIAH

Seven Group Bible Studies

Alec Motyer with Wendy S Robins

Series editor: Wendy S Robins

BIBLE SOCIETY
Stonehill Green, Westlea, Swindon SN5 7DG, England

First published 1987. Reprinted 1989, 1991.

British Library Cataloguing in Publication Data

Motyer, Alec
Nehemiah: seven group Bible studies—(Work with the Word)
1. Bible. O.T. Nehemiah—Study—Outlines, syllabi, etc.
I. Title II. Robins, Wendy S. III. Series 222'.806 BS1365.5

ISBN 0–564–03104–6

Designed and typeset by Nuprint Ltd, Harpenden, Herts AL5 4SE
Printed in Great Britain

Bible Societies exist to provide resources for Bible distribution and use. Bible Society in England and Wales (BFBS) is a member of the United Bible Societies, an international partnership working in over 150 countries. Their common aim is to reach all people with the Bible, or some part of it, in a language they can understand and at a price they can afford. Parts of the Bible have now been translated into approximately 1,800 languages. Bible Societies aim to help every church at every point where it uses the Bible. You are invited to share in this work by your prayers and gifts. The Bible Society in your country will be very happy to provide details of its activity.

CONTENTS

How to use this book

Before the group meeting

- Read the Introduction carefully. It is like a map of Nehemiah's story and it will give you a picture of the whole book before you go on to look at the individual parts. As you read look up the texts that are mentioned.
- Read through the material for the session. Each of the seven sessions contains a set of background notes or questions about the passage to be studied. These notes and questions are divided into six, so you can prepare one part of the passage on each of the six days between the meetings. But don't feel that you have to do the preparation in this way. Find out what suits you best and follow that system; as long as you prepare before the meeting it doesn't matter how you choose to do it.
- As you read through the passage for each session make some notes about anything that you want to ask about at the group meeting. Also note down what particularly strikes you about the passage and any points that you do not understand.

At the group meeting

- Take with you this book, a Bible, and a pen or pencil.
- Be prepared to discuss your thoughts and questions about the passage with the other members of the group. Don't worry if you think some of your ideas sound silly. The group is the place to try out your ideas and ask questions. Everyone will have them so try to learn from each other.
- Remember that everyone in the group will have things to say, or ask

questions about. It might be that you won't always be able to say everything you want. Don't be frustrated by this. It is very important that everyone feels able to say something and that no one tries to dominate the group. However, do be sure to take the opportunity to discuss those questions and thoughts that are uppermost in your mind.

For group leaders

The studies in this book are designed so they can be lead by a different person for each session if that is what the group wishes. Alternatively, it might be that two or three people will each lead a session, or that one person might lead them all. Whatever pattern of leadership the group uses it is important that the group leader for each session thinks about the following:

Before the meeting

- Make sure the room you will be meeting in is ready. You need to arrange the chairs so that everyone can see each other (be sure that there are enough chairs for everyone). Check also that there is enough lighting for everyone to see and that there is enough heating and ventilation, so that no one will freeze and no one will fall asleep because of the heat!

- Prepare for the session by working through it as suggested in the "How to Use" notes. You may find that you want to know more about Nehemiah. If so, you will find helpful articles in the following: *The Illustrated Bible Dictionary* (Inter-Varsity Press), *The Interpreter's Dictionary of the Bible* (Abingdon Press), *The Zondervan Pictorial Bible Dictionary* (Zondervan Press), *The Lion Handbook of the Bible* (Lion Books), *The New Bible Commentary Revised* (Inter-Varsity Press). *A Bible Commentary for Today* (Pickering and Inglis) will help you with fuller discussion of the text of Nehemiah, as will *Peake's Commentary on the Bible* (Van Nostrand Reinhold (UK) Co Ltd). For even greater detail, try *Ezra and Nehemiah*, by D Kidner (Inter-Varsity Press), and *I and II Chronicles, Ezra and Nehemiah* by P R Ackroyd (SCM Press).

- Work out approximately how much time you will be able to spend on each part of the session. Every group is different and the one to which you belong will have a mind and life of its own. You will probably find that far more group material has been included than you can get through. The leader should help the group choose which questions to tackle and, where appropriate, the order in which to do them. It is important to take the time to discuss members' questions and thoughts as a result of their reading during the week. So be certain to leave a time in the group session for this.

At the meeting

- If the group members do not know each other already encourage them to get to know each other's names.
- Allow a few minutes after everyone has arrived for people to become accustomed to each other.
- If it is appropriate for your group, open the meeting with prayer.
- Lead the group through the session, making sure that everyone who wishes to gets the opportunity to contribute. But try not to let any one person dominate the conversation (and be careful not to dominate it yourself!) Be aware of anyone who is especially quiet and gently try to draw them in.
- Close the meeting with prayer.
- At the end of the session confirm the date, time, and place of the next meeting and who is leading it.
- Encourage people to stay and chat over a cup of tea or coffee.

Introduction

The book of Nehemiah is a great story. Read it for enjoyment. It's about:

- One man and what he achieved for God.
- Teamwork and what can happen when people get united and excited in obeying God.
- Putting down foundations, keeping going even when it's hard work, and bringing the task to completion.
- Problems and difficulties (success did not come easily—at one point the work almost ground to a halt when the team lost its unity).

The story

Look at the story in the Bible. Don't spend very much time doing this, just get a general idea of what happens. Give special attention to the bits referred to below. If you find this daunting move on to the paragraph below headed "Background to the story".

Here are references to some of the important points in Nehemiah's story.

Nehemiah's story

1.1–4	Nehemiah was distressed by news from his homeland in Judah. So he decides to do something about re-building the city of Jerusalem.
1.11	His job as a wine steward made him quite important in the emperor's court.
2.6–8	Nehemiah gets royal support for his building project.
2.10	Local officials in Palestine are suspicious of Nehemiah and of what he intends to do.
2.17–18	The people of Jerusalem respond warmly to his call.
3.1–32	Nehemiah gets everyone working.
4.1–7	Stage one is completed.
6.1	Nearly complete.
6.15	The final touches.

But it was far from being as easy as this review would suggest. There were:

4.8–23	Threats from outside.
5.1–5	Divisions inside.
6.1–9	Pressures on Nehemiah himself.

In other words Nehemiah's task was earthy and hard!

Background to the story

Most people think that the Persian emperor was Artaxerxes 1. He lived between 464 and 423 BC. Nehemiah probably came to Jerusalem about 445 BC. Here are some of the important events that led up to this time:

586 BC Jerusalem was captured and destroyed by the Babylonian army. The people of Jerusalem were taken as prisoners to Babylon.

539 BC Babylon was captured by Cyrus the Persian. He ordered that all the prisoners, the Judaeans included, should return to their own lands.

538 BC The Judaeans returned to Jerusalem and began to set up home again.

By the time the events recorded in this book took place the Judaeans had been back in Jerusalem for about a century.

The story today

Nehemiah's story is true. It really happened. Jerusalem was in ruins. It needed somebody with a vision and real concern to get it re-built and Nehemiah set to work and got it done. When we are discouraged today Nehemiah's story can help us to get a different perspective on things.

Nehemiah set about building a city (chapters 1–6) and a community (chapters 7–13). In the New Testament this building work becomes a picture of personal and church growth. The Letter from Jude encourages the people to "keep on building yourselves up on your most sacred faith" (verse 20) and the Letter to the Ephesians tells them to "build up the Body of Christ" (4.12). We are not often expected to build city walls today, although we do sometimes have to build or restore the walls of a church! The important building work for today is in personal spiritual growth, numerical growth in the churches, and growth in fellowship. Nehemiah's story can offer us help with these things. The lessons he learned can give us pointers as we think about how we can grow as Christian people, how the numbers in our church can grow, and how the fellowship that we experience with others can deepen. I hope these sessions will give you the tools to help you discover what Nehemiah can mean for us.

Alec Motyer

SESSION ONE

REAL FOUNDATIONS

1 This is the account of what
Nehemiah son of Hacaliah accom-
plished.
In the month of Kislev in the
twentieth year that Artaxerxes was
emperor of Persia, I, Nehemiah, was in
Susa, the capital city. [2]Hanani, one of
my brothers, arrived from Judah with a
group of other men, and I asked them
about Jerusalem and about our fellow-
Jews who had returned from exile in
Babylonia. [3]They told me that those
who had survived and were back in the
homeland were in great difficulty and
that the foreigners who lived near by
looked down on them. They also told
me that the walls of Jerusalem were
still broken down and that the gates
had not been restored since the time
they were burnt. [4]When I heard all this,
I sat down and wept.
For several days I mourned and did
not eat. I prayed to God, [5]"LORD God of
Heaven! You are great, and we stand in
fear of you. You faithfully keep your
covenant with those who love you and
do what you command. [6]Look at me,
LORD, and hear my prayer, as I pray day
and night for your servants, the people
of Israel. I confess that we, the people
of Israel, have sinned. My ancestors
and I have sinned. [7]We have acted
wickedly against you and have not done
what you commanded. We have not
kept the laws which you gave us
through Moses, your servant.
[8]Remember now what you told
Moses: 'If you people of Israel are
unfaithful to me, I will scatter you
among the other nations. [9]But then if
you turn back to me and do what I have
commanded you, I will bring you back
to the place where I have chosen to be
worshipped, even though you are
scattered to the ends of the earth.'
10 "Lord, these are your servants,
your own people. You rescued them
by your great power and strength.
[11]Listen now to my prayer and to the
prayers of all your other servants who
want to honour you. Give me success
today and make the emperor merciful
to me."
In those days I was the emperor's
wine steward.

2 One day four months later, when
Emperor Artaxerxes was dining, I took
the wine to him. He had never seen
me look sad before, [2]so he asked,
"Why are you looking so sad? You
aren't ill, so it must be that you're
unhappy."
I was startled [3]and answered, "May
Your Majesty live for ever! How can I
help looking sad when the city where
my ancestors are buried is in ruins and
its gates have been destroyed by fire?"
4 The emperor asked, "What is it
that you want?"

I prayed to the God of Heaven, 5 and
then I said to the emperor, "If Your
Majesty is pleased with me and is willing to grant my request, let me go to
the land of Judah, to the city where my
ancestors are buried, so that I can rebuild the city."
6 The emperor, with the empress
sitting at his side, approved my
request. He asked me how long I
would be gone and when I would
return, and I told him.
7 Then I asked him to grant me the
favour of giving me letters to the
governors of West Euphrates
Province, instructing them to let me
travel to Judah. 8 I asked also for a letter
to Asaph, keeper of the royal forests,
instructing him to supply me with
timber for the gates of the fort that
guards the Temple, for the city walls,
and for the house I was to live in. The
emperor gave me all I asked for,
because God was with me.
9 The emperor sent some army
officers and a troop of horsemen with
me, and I made the journey to West
Euphrates. There I gave the emperor's
letters to the governors. 10 But
Sanballat, from the town of Beth
Horon, and Tobiah, an official in the
province of Ammon, heard that some-
one had come to work for the good of
the people of Israel, and they were
highly indignant.

Nehemiah 1.1—2.10

Nehemiah does not want the spotlight to fall on him. He plunges straight into the story without any personal introduction. His explanation of his actions is simple—read it for yourselves in verses 1–4.

Before the group meeting

Read the passage in six steps, if you wish, and then look at the thoughts and background information given below. This will help you to come to grips with the passage.

The decisive moment 1.1–3

v1 Kislev: The ninth of the twelve months in the Babylonian calendar. The equivalent of about mid-November to about mid-December in our calendar.

twentieth year: About 445 BC.

Susa: A royal city in south-west Persia about 150 miles north of the Persian Gulf.

v2 exile: See Introduction, p7

v3 walls...broken: This might refer to the destruction of the walls by the Babylonians in 586 BC. But if it does, it's hard to understand why Nehemiah is suddenly upset by it. It might be that Ezra 4.12 refers to an attempt to build the walls about twelve years before Nehemiah's story. If it does, then Nehemiah might have been upset at hearing this start had come to nothing.

The first foundation 1.4–7

Things to think about:

- How did Nehemiah react to the news about Jerusalem?
- What did he do?
- In what order did he do it?
- Why?
- What can you learn from this about the way you react to things now?

Continuing prayer 1.8–11

To think about:

- Nehemiah probably wanted things to happen quickly, but he was prepared to wait for God's timing. Can you think of examples from your own life when you wanted to race on with something, but had to wait for the right time?

At last 2.1–3

v2 unhappy: Literally "evil in heart". The emperor might have thought that Nehemiah was trying to poison him.

Prayer that works 2.4–7

To think about:

- Jerusalem had a reputation for being a place where rebellions started, so the emperor could easily have become alarmed by Nehemiah's request.
- Can you think of a time in your experience when you were certain that you had to do something even though it was a risk? What was it? How did it feel? What happened?

Storms ahead   2.8–10

v10 Writings outside the Bible tell us that Sanballat and Tobiah were men of local importance and power. It is possible that while Judah was without a governor they had been able to treat it as a part of their territory and gather money from it.

- What do verses 8 and 9 tell us about the way God answers prayer?

↳ He often accomplishes many purposes at one time.

At the group meeting

1. Spend some time discussing the reading that you have done during the week. Think about the questions you have considered and focus particularly on:

- Any problems raised.
- Any problems solved.
- Anything that spoke to you.

Make sure that everyone who wants to has the time to contribute their thoughts and ideas.

2. Nehemiah was in a unique position which he was able to use for God. In some way, however small, we all have unique opportunities and capacities. Take some time to make notes below about the opportunities and capacities that you have:

- At home ____________________
- At work ____________________
- Socially ____________________
- In church ____________________

Now, discuss these opportunities with other group members. Decide if you could make better use of them. If so, think about how you could do this and ask the group to support you as you try.

3. The Bible can teach us a lot about God. We can learn from Nehemiah's story. These questions will help you to see more clearly what you have been given the opportunity of learning.

   How is God described (1.5)?

   YHWH God of Heaven to be feared faithful.

   What does Nehemiah remind us that God has given to his people (1.7)?

   Laws via Moses

   How does God act towards his people (1.8–9)?

   He sends them away if they turn from Him, but if the repent he relents

What do these things mean to you today? Does anything that you have written strike a chord in you? Think about who God is, what he has given to his people, and how he acts. Are you ever conscious of these things? Make some notes below, then share your thoughts with the group.

4. What different aspects of prayer can you find examples of in the passage (1.2–11)?

   How can wc bring these different aspects of prayer into our own prayer life; either:

   - In our private prayers?
   - In our family prayers?
   - In our church prayers?

   Make some notes and then discuss them with the group.

Nehemiah seems to have put prayer first. Is this true for you? If so, how? If not, how could you begin to organize yourself so that this could happen?

Is it true for your church? What could your group do to make it true?

Discuss your thoughts and, where possible, make plans to implement them.

SESSION TWO
TEAM-WORK

11 I went on to Jerusalem, and for
three days 12 I did not tell anyone what
God had inspired me to do for Jerusalem. Then in the middle of the night I
got up and went out, taking a few of
my companions with me. The only
animal we took was the donkey that I
rode on. 13 It was still night as I left the
city through the Valley Gate on the
west and went south past Dragon's
Fountain to the Rubbish Gate. As I
went, I inspected the broken walls of
the city and the gates that had been
destroyed by fire. 14 Then on the east
side of the city I went north to the
Fountain Gate and the King's Pool. The
donkey I was riding could not find any
path through the rubble, 15 so I went
down into the valley of the Kidron and
rode along, looking at the wall. Then I
returned the way I had come and went
back into the city through the Valley
Gate.
16 None of the local officials knew
where I had been or what I had been
doing. So far I had not said anything to
any of my fellow-Jews—the priests,
the leaders, the officials, or anyone else
who would be taking part in the work.
17 But now I said to them, "See what
trouble we are in because Jerusalem is
in ruins and its gates are destroyed!
Let's rebuild the city walls and put an
end to our disgrace." 18 And I told them
how God had been with me and helped
me, and what the emperor had said to
me.
They responded, "Let's start rebuilding!" And they got ready to start
the work.
19 When Sanballat, Tobiah, and an
Arab named Geshem heard what we
were planning to do, they laughed at
us and said, "What do you think you're
doing? Are you going to rebel against
the emperor?"
20 I answered, "The God of Heaven
will give us success. We are his servants, and we are going to start building. But you have no right to any
property in Jerusalem, and you have
no share in its traditions."

3 This is how the city wall was rebuilt.
The High Priest Eliashib and his fellow-
priests rebuilt the Sheep Gate, dedicated it, and put the gates in place.
They dedicated the wall as far as the
Tower of the Hundred and the Tower
of Hananel.
2 The men of Jericho built the next
section.
Zaccur son of Imri built the next
section.
3 The clan of Hassenaah built the
Fish Gate. They put the beams and the
gates in place, and put in the bolts and
bars for locking the gate.
4 Meremoth, the son of Uriah and
grandson of Hakkoz, built the next

section.

Meshullam, the son of Berechiah and grandson of Meshezabel, built the next section.

Zadok son of Baana built the next section.

5 The men of Tekoa built the next section, but the leading men of the town refused to do the manual labour assigned to them by the supervisors.

6 Joiada son of Paseah and Meshullam son of Besodeiah rebuilt Jeshanah Gate. They put the beams and the gates in place, and put in the bolts and bars for locking the gate.

7 Melatiah from Gibeon, Jadon from Meronoth, and the men of Gibeon and Mizpah built the next section, as far as the residence of the governor of West Euphrates.

8 Uzziel son of Harhaiah, a goldsmith, built the next section.

Hananiah, a maker of perfumes, built the next section, as far as Broad Wall.

9 Rephaiah son of Hur, ruler of half the Jerusalem District, built the next section.

10 Jedaiah son of Harumaph built the next section, which was near his own house.

Hattush son of Hashabneiah built the next section.

11 Malchijah son of Harim and Hasshub son of Pahath Moab built both the next section and the Tower of the Ovens.

12 Shallum son of Hallohesh, ruler of the other half of the Jerusalem District, built the next section. (His daughters helped with the work.)

13 Hanun and the inhabitants of the city of Zanoah rebuilt the Valley Gate. They put the gates in place, put in the bolts and the bars for locking the gate, and repaired the wall for 440 metres, as far as the Rubbish Gate.

14 Malchijah son of Rechab, ruler of the Beth Haccherem District, rebuilt the Rubbish Gate. He put the gates in place, and put in the bolts and the bars for locking the gate.

15 Shallum son of Colhozeh, ruler of the Mizpah District, rebuilt the Fountain Gate. He covered the gateway, put the gates in place, and put in the bolts and the bars. At the Pool of Shelah he built the wall next to the royal garden, as far as the steps leading down from David's City.

16 Nehemiah son of Azbuk, ruler of half the Bethzur District, built the next section, as far as David's tomb, the pool, and the barracks.

17 The following Levites rebuilt the next several sections of the wall:

Rehum son of Bani built the next section;

Hashabiah, ruler of half the Keilah District, built the next section on behalf of his district;

18 Bavvai son of Henadad, ruler of the other half of the Keilah District, built the next section;

19 Ezer son of Jeshua, ruler of Mizpah, built the next section in front of the armoury, as far as the place where the wall turns;

20 Baruch son of Zabbai built the next section, as far as the entrance to the house of the High Priest Eliashib;

21 Meremoth, the son of Uriah and grandson of Hakkoz, built the next section, up to the far end of Eliashib's house.

22 The following priests rebuilt the next several sections of the wall:

Priests from the area around Jerusalem built the next section;

23 Benjamin and Hasshub built the next section, which was in front of their houses;

Azariah, the son of Maaseiah and grandson of Ananiah, built the next section, which was in front of his house;

24 Binnui son of Henadad built the next section, from Azariah's house to the corner of the wall;

25–26 Palal son of Uzai built the next section, beginning at the corner of the wall and the tower of the upper palace near the court of the guard;

Pedaiah son of Parosh built the next

section, to a point on the east near the Water Gate and the tower guarding the Temple. (This was near that part of the city called Ophel, where the temple workmen lived.)

27 The men of Tekoa built the next section, their second one, from a point opposite the large tower guarding the Temple as far as the wall near Ophel.

28 A group of priests built the next section, going north from the Horse Gate, each one building in front of his own house.

29 Zadok son of Immer built the next section, which was in front of his house.

Shemaiah son of Shecaniah, keeper of the East Gate, built the next section.

30 Hananiah son of Shelemiah and Hanun, the sixth son of Zalaph, built the next section, their second one.

Meshullam son of Berechiah built the next section, which was in front of his house.

31 Malchijah, a goldsmith, built the next section, as far as the building used by the temple workmen and the merchants, which was by the Miphkad Gate, near the room on top of the north-east corner of the wall.

32 The goldsmiths and the merchants built the last section, from the room at the corner as far as the Sheep Gate.

Nehemiah 2.11—3.32

Here again Nehemiah doesn't draw attention to what he is doing. He makes sure of what needs doing before he lets people know his plans and then gathers a team of workers around him.

Before the group meeting

Read the passage in six steps, if you wish, and then look at the thoughts and background information given below. This will help you to come to grips with the passage.

Dead of night 2.11–15

Follow Nehemiah round the city on the map on page 17. Verse 15 reads as if Nehemiah turned back on his route. But it can be understood as saying that when Nehemiah "went down into the valley" he was able to pick his way round along the line of what was to be the north wall. Going this way he would be able to get back to the Valley Gate, from which he had started.

Enthusiasm 2.16–18

Once the people who lived in Jerusalem were prompted to see what a state the place was in they responded with enthusiasm to the idea of repairing it.

v16 "Fellow Jews" should really read "fellow Judaeans". The religion we know as Judaism had not yet developed.

v18 Two different powers are mentioned. Note which Nehemiah puts first.

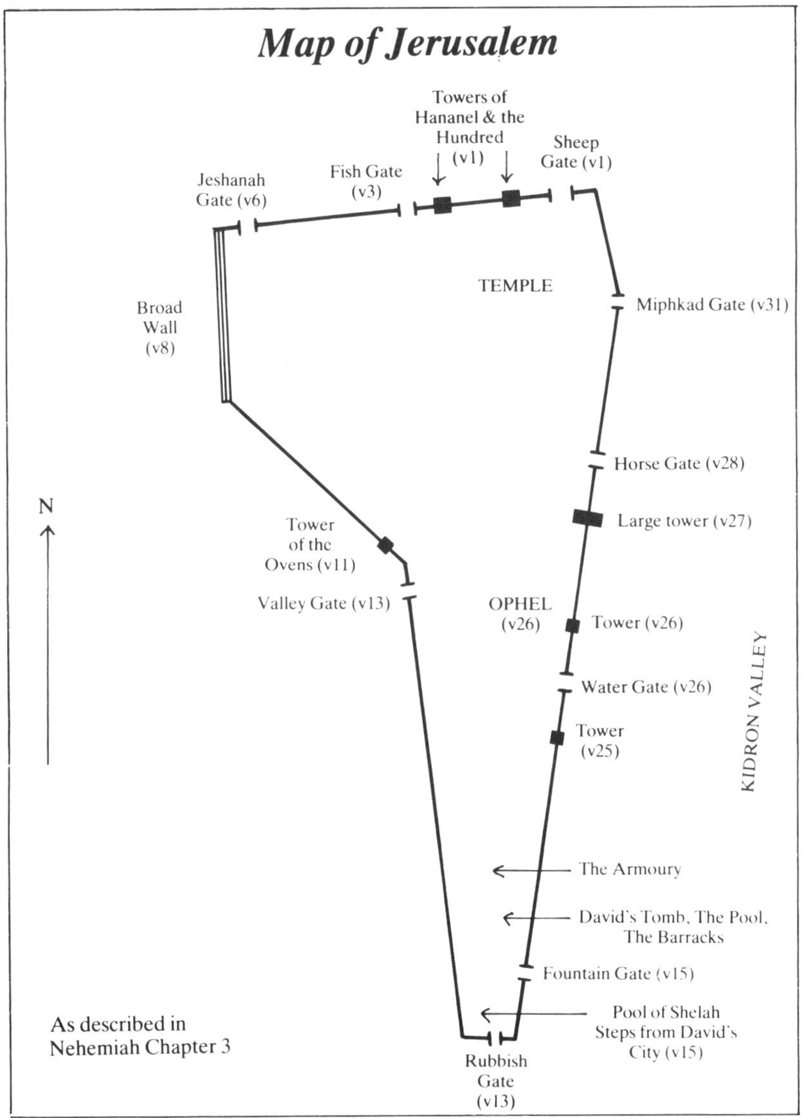

Mockery 2.19–20

God was with the builders but this was no guarantee of a trouble-free life. The hostility (v10) becomes mockery (v19) and another local man of importance joins the opposition.

v19 rebel	This accusation is the real sting in the mockery. Nehemiah is concerned only for the dignity of the city, but walls are always a defensive weapon. Emperors were very sensitive about any possibility of rebellion (see, for instance, Ezra 4.20–22).
v20 God of Heaven	Nehemiah seemed to use this title when he wanted help against great odds—in 1.4 as he realized all that there was to be done and in 2.4 when talking to the emperor.
no share	God's work must be done by his true and committed people.

It takes all sorts 3.1–5

The people who undertook the task of building the wall were not builders by trade. Look later at the list of different trades and crafts mentioned. Everyone seemed willing to try because that's what they believed God wanted. Only one group felt themselves to be too good to get their hands dirty (v5). Chapter three is not just a list of places, it is a statement of commitment; the wall is made of stone, but represents personal effort and sacrifice.

- Can you think of any examples of personal effort and sacrifice in your Christian community? What are they and what effect did they have on other people?

Co-operation 3.7–10

Different parts of the wall were built by different people and eventually all the parts joined up. In these verses we can see the implicit statement "I am prepared to work beside you". Co-operation is the key word.

- Can you think of any areas in your life in which you do not co-operate with others as well as you might? Think about what you might do about this.

Co-ordination 3.29–32

With so many people working on the wall at different times everything had to be made to fit together properly. The stones had to mesh together, which meant that the teams of workers had to mesh too. The task of co-ordination must have been huge, but it was also one of the most important elements in making the whole project work. See the map on p20.

Each team relied on the others to help them make the wall stand.

At the group meeting

1. Spend some time, as last session, discussing the reading you have done during the week. Think about the questions you have considered and focus particularly on:

   - Any problems raised.
   - Any problems solved.
   - Anything that spoke to you.

   Make sure that everyone who wants to has the time to contribute their thoughts and ideas.

2. Nehemiah was a very careful planner:

2.7–8	He seemed already to know what he'd need to ask from the emperor.
2.12–17	His arrival and the spreading of his idea is carefully ordered.
3.1–32	He must have had a detailed master plan for the wall showing where it would be built and how the teams would work together.

   - What kinds of forward planning and thinking happens in your church? Think particularly about the areas of work that you help in. Is planning taken seriously? Are plans made well enough in advance? Are they detailed enough, or are too many things left to chance?
   - How are plans communicated to those outside the planning group? Are they clear?
   - Are there improvements that could be made in planning or communication? How can these happen?

Rebuilding the walls

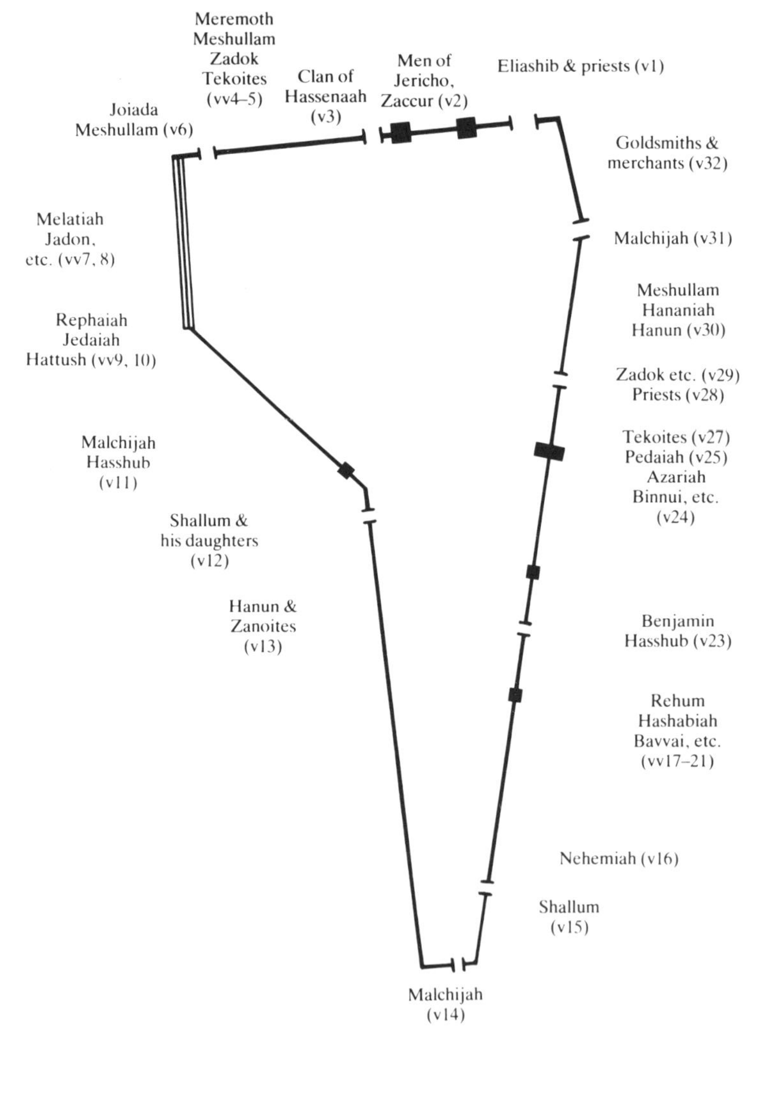

3. There are twenty-five individuals named and then about fourteen other groups, trades, and professions. List some of them—look for example at verses 1, 2, 3, and 5.

   There is something for everyone to do. Jesus taught this too—look at Matthew 20.1–7, and at what Paul wrote in 1 Corinthians 12.14–21 and Ephesians 4.7.

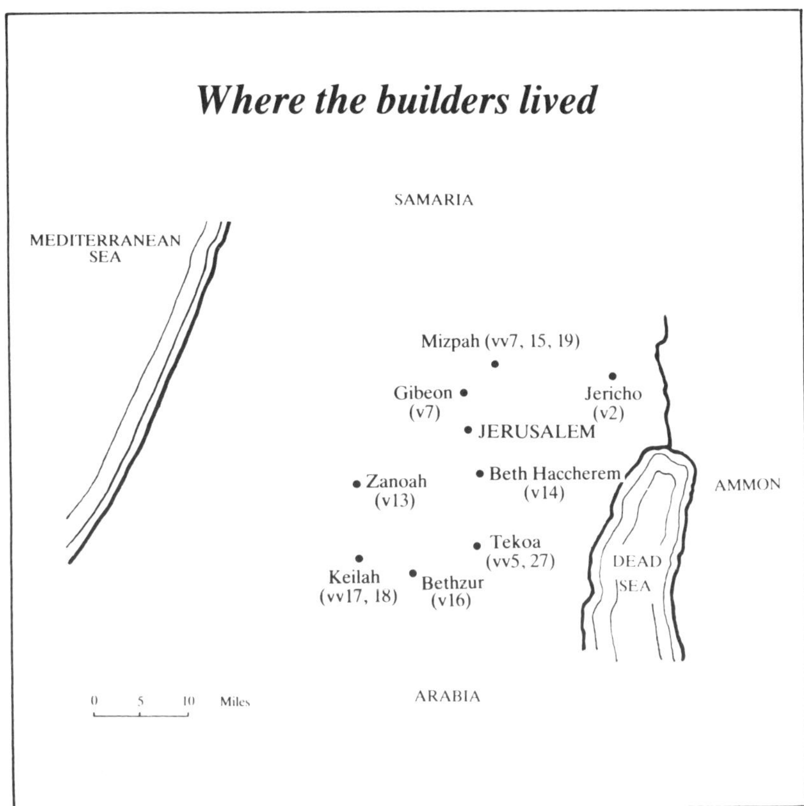

Think about:

- What it involved for the goldsmith or perfume maker to turn builder. (v8)
- What was necessary for those who lived a long way away to be involved (see map above).
- What principles this gives us which we can apply to our building tasks. These might be actual bricks and mortar building tasks or those involved in building the community within your Christian group and the world around it.

4. Co-operation and co-ordination are the two most important features of chapter three. But it's not always easy. Did it matter whether or not the builders co-operated with each other?

   Would the wall have been built without co-operation and co-ordination?

   Look at Acts 15.36–41. Did Paul and Barnabas take the best possible actions? What else might they have done?

   In Philippians 4.2 we can see that Paul and Barnabas were not the only people to have problems. Read Galatians 2.11–14 too.

   - Is division ever justified? If so, in what circumstances? If not, why not?
   - What sort of things can make working together difficult? Share some of your experiences with the group (be honest if there are difficulties within the group, but be sensitive).
   - How can the group work together to help each other with any difficulties?

SESSION THREE

STANDING TOGETHER

1 When Sanballat heard that we Jews
had begun rebuilding the wall, he was
furious and began to ridicule us. [2]In
front of his companions and the
Samaritan troops he said, "What do
these miserable Jews think they're
doing? Do they intend to rebuild the
city? Do they think that by offering
sacrifices they can finish the work in
one day? Can they make building
stones out of heaps of burnt rubble?"
3 Tobiah was standing there beside
him, and he added, "What kind of wall
could they ever build? Even a fox could
knock it down!"
4 I prayed, "Listen to them mocking
us, O God! Let their ridicule fall on their
own heads. Let them be robbed of
everything they have, and let them be
taken as prisoners to a foreign land.
[5]Don't forgive the evil they do and don't
forget their sins, for they have insulted
us who are building."
6 So we went on rebuilding the wall,
and soon it was half its full height,
because the people were eager to
work.
7 Sanballat, Tobiah, and the people

of Arabia, Ammon, and Ashdod heard
that we were making progress in rebuilding the wall of Jerusalem and that
the gaps in the wall were being closed,
and they were very angry. 8So they all
plotted together to come and attack
Jerusalem and create confusion, 9but
we prayed to our God and kept men on
guard against them day and night.
10 The people of Judah had a song
they sang:
"We grow weak carrying burdens;
There's so much rubble to take away.
How can we build the wall today?"
11 Our enemies thought we would
not see them or know what was
happening until they were already upon
us, killing us and putting an end to our
work. 12But time after time Jews who
were living among our enemies came
to warn us of the plans our enemies
were making against us. 13So I armed
the people with swords, spears, and
bows, and stationed them by clans
behind the wall, wherever it was still
unfinished.
14 I saw that the people were
worried, so I said to them and to their
leaders and officials, "Don't be afraid
of our enemies. Remember how great
and terrifying the Lord is, and fight for
your fellow-countrymen, your children,
your wives, and your homes." 15Our
enemies heard that we had found out
what they were plotting, and they
realized that God had defeated their
plans. Then all of us went back to
rebuilding the wall.
16 From then on half my men
worked and half stood guard, wearing
coats of armour and armed with spears,
shields, and bows. And our leaders
gave their full support to the people
17who were rebuilding the wall. Even
those who carried building materials
worked with one hand and kept a
weapon in the other, 18and everyone
who was building kept a sword
strapped to his waist. The man who
was to sound the alarm on the bugle
stayed with me. 19 I told the people and
their officials and leaders, "The work is
spread out over such a distance that
we are widely separated from one
another on the wall. 20If you hear the
bugle, gather round me. Our God will
fight for us." 21 So every day, from
dawn until the stars came out at night,
half of us worked on the wall, while the
other half stood guard with spears.
22 During this time I told the men in
charge that they and all their helpers
had to stay in Jerusalem at night, so
that we could guard the city at night as
well as work in the daytime. 23I didn't
take off my clothes even at night,
neither did any of my companions nor
my servants nor my bodyguard. And
we all kept our weapons to hand.

Nehemiah 4.1–23

Last session we saw how the workers co-ordinated their work and co-operated together. Now we shall see that it didn't all go smoothly. There was a great deal of opposition and the animosity and mockery of chapter two becomes the gathering of forces which leads to an offensive alliance and the threat of attack.

Before the group meeting

Read the passage in six steps:

Mobilization 4.1–3

What were Sanballat, his companions, the Samaritan army, and Tobiah all doing together in one place? We can imagine Sanballat calling a conference to consider the question of Jerusalem. In fact, we could almost imagine the army as the guard of honour there to meet Tobiah. Verses 2 and 3 might even be bits of Sanballat's speech of welcome and Tobiah's reply.

- Think about how it must have felt to be ridiculed like that and what you might have done in response.

Answering the mockery 4.4–6

v4 I prayed	These words are not in the Hebrew, where the ridicule is immediately followed by the words of the prayer, making the contrast between the two much starker.
ridicule... robbed... prisoners	According to Jewish Law (Deuteronomy 19.18–19) people who made false accusations should receive as punishment what would have been received by the ones they accused.
v5 don't forgive	Nehemiah is aware of God's incredible mercy so he reminds him that if Sanballat isn't stopped the wall will not get built and Nehemiah believes God wants Jerusalem to have walls again.

- Having resorted to prayer how else did Nehemiah and his people reply to Sanballat?

Fighting and fear 4.7–10

Attack is imminent (vs7–8) but everyone in the city is despondent. But Nehemiah isn't defeated.

- What is planned to beat the attack (v9)?
- How does the verse help us to understand the proper balance between prayer and action?

Don't be afraid...remember 4.11–15

Once again the order in which Nehemiah places things is important. What is the first armour he offers to his people as they face attack?

- Can we learn anything from this for ourselves? If we look towards God more and remember his strength would we find our despondency and defeatism disappearing?

United we stand 4.16–20

Everyone is committed to the task ahead of them: Nehemiah, his men, the leaders, and the work-force itself. Nehemiah believed that God was going to help them finish their task too.

God is always there to support his people (see Romans 8.31ff.) But Nehemiah knew that unity within God's people was important as well. It's only if we have unity that we can stand against attack. See Philippians 1.27–28.

No relaxation 4.21–23

v21 This reminds us that Nehemiah commits his own men to work as hard as everyone else. (In v16 his men were working also.) He gets involved himself.

- Can we learn anything about leadership from this? What?

v22 Look at the map on p21 to see from how far the people came to help the re-building programme.

v23 Notice the tension and alertness in the air.

At the group meeting

1. Talk about anything that has been raised in your reading during the week. Discuss together the answers that you gave to some of the questions. Think back to last week's meeting. Have you found anything helpful that you decided to do as a result of your discussion about people with whom you find it difficult to co-operate? Can the group do anything else to help you?

2. Nehemiah's thoughts promptly turn to God whatever is happening to him. He has a fresh sense of God as present, alert, and active. How does this show itself in:

v3–4 ______________________________

v8–9 ______________________________

v14 ______________________________

v15 ______________________________

Do you think it's possible for us to develop a similar sense of God's presence? How? Is there something that you find especially helpful for you to be *aware of God*? Tell it to the group.

Here are twelve things which Christians find helpful. Rank them 1–12 (1 as the most helpful) showing which you find most helpful or which you think you would find most helpful if you were to do any of them:

Meditation ______________

Bible reading ______________

Memorizing Bible verses or hymns ______________

A time early in the morning for Bible reading and prayer ______________

Developing friendships both in and out of the Christian community ______________

Church service ______________

Social action in the community ______________

Meeting with other Christians to pray ______________

Being with other Christians ______________

Keeping a (manageable) prayer list ______________

Saying thank you to God ______________

Reading Christian books ______________

3. What do you think about Nehemiah's prayer in verses 4 and 5? Is it a problem to you?

   Jesus asked his father to forgive those who crucified him (Luke 23.34), saying, "Forgive them, Father! They don't know what they are doing." Why do you think Jesus and Nehemiah prayed as they did? Why do you answer as you do? Do you think it is ever right to pray against people, circumstances, etc? If so, what can be asked for? If not, why not?

4. Nehemiah's building work was assaulted. Remind yourself of the ways in which this happened. Look at verses 1, 8, and 11.

   Are there equivalents today in relation to:

   - Our personal spiritual growth?
   - Growth in fellowship with our Christian community?
   - Numerical growth?

   What are they?

   What can we learn from Nehemiah about guarding against these things?

SESSION FOUR

STRESS, STRAIN, SUCCESS

5 Some time later many of the people,
both men and women, began to com-
plain against their fellow-Jews. [2]Some
said, "We have large families, we need
corn to keep us alive."
3 Others said, "We have had to
mortgage our fields and vineyards and
houses to get enough corn to keep us
from starving."
4 Still others said, "We had to
borrow money to pay the royal tax on
our fields and vineyards. [5]We are of
the same race as our fellow-Jews.
Aren't our children just as good as

theirs? But we have to make slaves of our children. Some of our daughters have already been sold as slaves. We are helpless because our fields and vineyards have been taken away from us."

6 When I heard their complaints, I was angry [7]and decided to act. I denounced the leaders and officials of the people and told them, "You are oppressing your brothers!"

I called a public assembly to deal with the problem [8]and said, "As far as we have been able, we have been buying back our Jewish brothers who had to sell themselves to foreigners. Now you are forcing your own brothers to sell themselves to you, their fellow-Jews!" The leaders were silent and could find nothing to say.

9 Then I said, "What you are doing is wrong! You ought to obey God and do what's right. Then you would not give our enemies, the Gentiles, any reason to ridicule us. [10]I have let the people borrow money and corn from me, and so have my companions and the men who work for me. Now let's give up all our claims to repayment. [11]Cancel all the debts they owe you—money or corn or wine or olive-oil. And give them back their fields, vineyards, olive-groves, and houses at once!"

12 The leaders replied, "We'll do as you say. We'll give the property back and not try to collect the debts."

I called in the priests and made the leaders swear in front of them to keep the promise they had just made. [13]Then I took off the sash I was wearing round my waist and shook it out. "This is how God will shake any of you who don't keep your promise," I said. "God will take away your houses and everything you own, and will leave you with nothing."

Everyone who was present said, "Amen!" and praised the LORD. And the leaders kept their promise.

14 During all the twelve years that I was governor of the land of Judah, from the twentieth year that Artaxerxes was emperor until his thirty-second year, neither my relatives nor I ate the food I was entitled to have as governor. [15]Every governor who had been in office before me had been a burden to the people and had demanded forty silver coins a day for food and wine. Even their servants had oppressed the people. But I acted differently, because I honoured God. [16]I put all my energy into rebuilding the wall and did not acquire any property. Everyone who worked for me joined in the rebuilding. [17]I regularly fed at my table a hundred and fifty of the Jewish people and their leaders, besides all the people who came to me from the surrounding nations. [18]Every day I served one ox, six of the best sheep, and many chickens, and every ten days I provided a fresh supply of wine. But I knew what heavy burdens the people had to bear, so I did not claim the allowance that the governor is entitled to.

19 I pray you, O God, remember to my credit everything that I have done for this people.

6 Sanballat, Tobiah, Geshem, and the rest of our enemies heard that we had finished building the wall and that there were no gaps left in it, although we still had not set up the gates in the gateways. [2]So Sanballat and Geshem sent me a message, suggesting that I meet with them in one of the villages in the Plain of Ono. This was a trick of theirs to try to harm me. [3]I sent messengers to say to them, "I am doing important work and can't go down there. I am not going to let the work stop just to go and see you."

4 They sent me the same message four times, and each time I sent them the same reply.

5 Then Sanballat sent one of his servants to me with a fifth message, this one in the form of an unsealed letter. [6]It read:

> "Geshem tells me that a rumour is going round among the neighbouring peoples that you and the

Jewish people intend to revolt and
that this is why you are rebuilding
the wall. He also says you plan to
make yourself king 7 and that you
have arranged for some prophets to
proclaim in Jerusalem that you are
the king of Judah. His Majesty is
certain to hear about this, so I
suggest that you and I meet to talk
the situation over."
8 I sent a reply to him: "Nothing of
what you are saying is true. You have
made it all up yourself."
9 They were trying to frighten us
into stopping work. I prayed, "But
now, God, make me strong!"
10 About this time I went to visit
Shemaiah, the son of Delaiah and
grandson of Mehetabel, who was un-
able to leave his house. He said to me,
"You and I must go and hide together
in the Holy Place of the Temple and
lock the doors, because they are com-
ing to kill you. Any night now they will
come to kill you."
11 I answered, "I'm not the kind of
man that runs and hides. Do you think I
would try to save my life by hiding in
the Temple? I won't do it."
12 When I thought it over, I realized
that God had not spoken to Shemaiah,
but that Tobiah and Sanballat had
bribed him to give me this warning.
13 They hired him to frighten me into
sinning, so that they could ruin my
reputation and humiliate me.
14 I prayed, "God, remember what
Tobiah and Sanballat have done and
punish them. Remember that woman
Nodiah and all the other prophets who
tried to frighten me."
15 After fifty-two days of work the
entire wall was finished on the twenty-
fifth day of the month of Elul. 16 When
our enemies in the surrounding nations
heard this, they realized that they had
lost face, since everyone knew that
the work had been done with God's
help.
17 During all this time the Jewish
leaders had been in correspondence
with Tobiah. 18 Many people in Judah
were on his side because of his Jewish
father-in-law, Shecaniah son of Arah.
In addition, his son Jehohanan had
married the daughter of Meshullam
son of Berechiah. 19 People would talk
in front of me about all the good deeds
Tobiah had done and would tell him
everything I said. And he kept sending
me letters to try to frighten me.

Nehemiah 5.1—6.19

Two more problems are revealed in this passage; disunity among the builders and Sanballat's attempt to discredit Nehemiah.

Before the group meeting

The haves and have-nots 5.1–5

v2 This probably refers to daily wage-earners who had given up their jobs to come and build. Having lost their incomes they need community help to survive.

v3 It's quite likely that a bad season had caused the price of corn to rise. So even those who owned property were having a hard time surviving.

v4	The taxes that people were forced to pay were very harsh.
v5	Other Judaeans were cashing in on the situation and making money out of it.

Nehemiah's community was becoming two communities and division could be disasterous.

Leading by example 5.14–19

Notice Nehemiah's behaviour and his reasons for it (vs15 and 18).

- What can we learn from Nehemiah's unselfishness?
- How do you respond to verse 19? Does it seem right to ask God to remember things to our credit?

Dedication 6.1–3

At times this story reads like a film about gangland in-fights! Here we can see the beginning of a plot to help Nehemiah disappear!

v2 Plain of Ono	This was to the north of the province of Judah, in the borderland between Judah and Samaria.
a trick	We are told the reason given for the invitation, but Nehemiah spots that it is a trick. His reply is not in terms of his own cleverness, but reflects his determination to complete the work that God has given him.

Think about Nehemiah's reply to Sanballat and Geshem:

- Does this say anything about how we can protect ourselves from temptation? If so, what?

Clear conscience 6.5–8

v5 unsealed letter	Leaving a letter unsealed was a deliberate way of making certain that its contents became widely known. The intrigue continues. Sanballat starts a whisper which could discredit Nehemiah and frighten the people with the thought that they are being "conned" into rebellion. Nehemiah's reply to Sanballat's letter is a plain assertion of a clear conscience. Is there anything about which your conscience is not absolutely

clear? How does this affect you? What can you do about it?

v9 Notice that Nehemiah turns to prayer again. He asks for further help as the going gets tough. Do you ever find yourself doing that. In what situations?

God cannot lie 6.10–13

Sanballat mentioned prophets in his letter to Nehemiah (v7) and then uses one, Shemaiah, to try to frighten Nehemiah and provide the opportunity for murder.

It was a cunning idea to try to use one of Nehemiah's strengths—his devotion to listening to the preaching of God's prophets—to beat him. But Nehemiah isn't fooled.

v11 Literally, "and who is there like me who may go into the Temple and live?" Nehemiah is not a priest and so he has no right to enter the Temple. To do so might lead to him being hurt, banished, or even killed (see 2 Chronicles 26.16–21).

v12 How do you think Nehemiah knew that God had not spoken to Shemaiah?

Strength in silence 6.15–19

Nehemiah does not try to prove or defend himself in the face of the leaders. He simply accepted that what was happening was a fact and didn't worry too much about it. Try to think of situations in which you face a choice about how to respond to injustice and to threats to yourself and others. What do you do? Is there anything to be learned from Nehemiah's behaviour? What?

At the group meeting

1. Look back over the readings since last session. Focus on:

- Any problems raised.
- Any problems solved.
- Anything that spoke to you.

2. The different facets of God's people are set against each other. Some wanted to see the wall built, others didn't. Some had plenty of food, others had none. Against this background intrigues flourished.

   Today, we have many different denominations and groups in the Christian church and sometimes even disagreements within our local Christian community.

   Should local Christians and churches try to do anything about denominational divisions? What? How?

   When there are disagreements within a particular church group what can we do? Is it important that we try to avoid conflict or can it be constructive at times?

3. The lack of food, need for temporary financial help, and real poverty that Nehemiah's people experienced are still problems today. In 5.6 we read that Nehemiah "heard their complaints (and) was angry".

   Are there world or local needs that make you feel really concerned? What are they?

   Is your church trying to do anything about these needs? Should it be? What could, or is, being done?

   Many churches and individuals give more to missionary work or to work concerned with social issues. What should be the balance between these two types of giving?

   How can we become aware of special, temporary, and desperate needs within our Christian community? How can we help deal with them?

4. Nehemiah worked effectively against the plots around him. How can we be equally effective against things we feel are wrong?

   - Take an issue of international importance, e.g. the failure of governments to take world hunger seriously, or the arms race.

   - Take a local issue, e.g. the availability of pornographic literature, videos, and films; racial prejudice, etc.

Look at Nehemiah's actions, especially in 5.6–7, and plan a course of action that will register your feelings about the issue and attempt to influence others and change the situation.

SESSION FIVE

THE PEOPLE AND THE BOOK

1 By the seventh month the people of
Israel were all settled in their towns.
On the first day of that month they all
assembled in Jerusalem, in the square
just inside the Water Gate. They asked
Ezra, the priest and scholar of the Law
which the LORD had given Israel
through Moses, to get the book of the
Law. 2So Ezra brought it to the place
where the people had gathered—men,
women, and the children who were
old enough to understand. 3There in
the square by the gate he read the Law
to them from dawn until noon, and
they all listened attentively.
4 Ezra was standing on a wooden
platform that had been built for the
occasion. The following men stood at
his right: Mattithiah, Shema, Anaiah,
Uriah, Hilkiah, and Maaseiah; and the
following stood at his left: Pedaiah,
Mishael, Malchijah, Hashum,
Hashbaddanah, Zechariah, and
Meshullam.
5 As Ezra stood there on the platform
high above the people, they all kept
their eyes fixed on him. As soon as he
opened the book, they all stood up.
6Ezra said, "Praise the LORD, the great
God!"
All the people raised their arms in
the air and answered, "Amen! Amen!"
They knelt in worship, with their faces
to the ground.
7 Then they rose and stood in their
places, and the following Levites
explained the Law to them: Jeshua,
Bani, Sherebiah, Jamin, Akkub,
Shabbethai, Hodiah, Maaseiah, Kelita,
Azariah, Jozabad, Hanan, and Pelaiah.
8They gave an oral translation of God's
Law and explained it so that the people
could understand it.
9 When the people heard what the
Law required, they were so moved that
they began to cry. So Nehemiah, who
was the governor, Ezra, the priest and
scholar of the Law, and the Levites
who were explaining the Law told all
the people, "This day is holy to the
LORD your God, so you are not to
mourn or cry. 10Now go home and have
a feast. Share your food and wine with
those who haven't enough. Today is
holy to our Lord, so don't be sad. The
joy that the LORD gives you will make
you strong."
11 The Levites went about calming
the people and telling them not to be
sad on such a holy day. 12So all the
people went home and ate and drank
joyfully and shared what they had with
others, because they understood what
had been read to them.
13 The next day the heads of the
clans, together with the priests and

the Levites, went to Ezra to study the
teachings of the Law. [14]They discovered that the Law, which the LORD
gave through Moses, ordered the
people of Israel to live in temporary
shelters during the Festival of Shelters.
[15]So they gave the following instructions and sent them all through Jerusalem and the other cities and towns:
"Go out to the hills and get branches
from pines, olives, myrtles, palms, and
other trees to make shelters according
to the instructions written in the Law."
16 So the people got branches and
built shelters on the flat roofs of their
houses, in their yards, in the temple
courtyard, and in the public squares by
the Water Gate and by the Ephraim
Gate. [17]All the people who had come
back from captivity built shelters and
lived in them. This was the first time it
had been done since the days of
Joshua son of Nun, and everybody was
excited and happy. [18]From the first day
of the festival to the last they read a
part of God's Law every day. They
celebrated for seven days, and on the
eighth day there was a closing ceremony, as required in the Law.

Nehemiah 8.1–18

Chapter seven tells us how Nehemiah turns his attention from building the city—once the walls are finished—to building the community. The chapter is concerned with birthright. Some people did not have the right to live within the walls. Nehemiah said that in order to do this, people had to give proof of their ancestry.

The apostle Paul expresses the same idea when he speaks of those who believe in Christ as citizens of heaven (Philippians 3.20) with names in God's book of the living (Philippians 4.3).

Chapter eight tells us that having settled who can live in the city Nehemiah turns his attention once again to consider the kind of life that the community should live.

Before the group meeting

The book is brought out 8.1–3

The first community action to be recorded is that of calling for the book of the Law and placing it at the centre of community life.

v1 Law	This was the name applied to the first five books of the Old Testament, also called "The Books of Moses". It was given to God's people to help them live as God wanted.

The people put the part of the Bible that they had at the centre of their life and were guided by it. We have the whole book; do we put that at the centre of our community?

The book is opened 8.4–6

By standing when the book was opened the people acknowledged the dignity and authority of the book. But Ezra praised God who gave them the book and not the book itself.

Do we ever praise the object rather than God himself? With what kinds of things? What do you think is the result of this?

The book is explained 8.7–9

v8 translation The Law was written in Hebrew but in Babylon the Jews had adopted Aramaic as the language for daily life. Because of this a translation was necessary. This verse probably means "They read God's Law and then translated it, explaining what it meant".

v9 began to cry This probably means that hearing the words of God's Law made the people realize they had done things that were wrong and for which they were sorry. But there are times to be sorry and times to be glad as Nehemiah points out.

The people understand 8.10–12

These are joyful verses. Verses 10 and 11 link joy and holiness and verse 12 traces the root of the joy. What is it? Have there been times when you have felt particularly joyful? When were they? What made you feel like that?

The people obey 8.13–15

v13 A study group is set up.

v14 Their studies lead them to a specific command which they obey.

Look up the Festival of Shelters: Leviticus 23.34–36, 39–43, and Deuteronomy 31.10–13.

What things are important about the Festival of Shelters?

The feast is kept 8.16–18

Imagine what it must have been like to celebrate this festival. Think about the things they were remembering. Are there important things that God has done in your life or those of people you know that it would be good to set aside a special time to remember? What kinds of things? How could you make sure you don't forget things as the Judaeans did?

At the group meeting

1. Once again focus on the reading that group members have done between the sessions. Give everyone who wants to a chance to explain their responses to the readings and questions.

2. Make a list of the things that we are told about the book of the Law. Then list the things that are said about Scripture as a whole in 2 Timothy 3.16–17 and 2 Peter 1.20–21.

   respected
   required explanation
   moving

   God breathed
   useful for teaching, rebuking, correcting and training in righteousness
   Not of man's will but of God.

   Jesus valued the Scriptures too. See how he refers to and uses them in the following examples:

   Matthew 5.17–20 Nothing of the law will pass away until judgement – J is fullfillment

   Matthew 15.1–9; 19.4–6 Word of God above tradition appealed to as final arbitor

   Matthew 26.47–56 what God has written must come to pass – J ordered his life by the word.

   Luke 10.25–29 ________

   Luke 24.27 ________

   Luke 24.45–49 ________

   What can we learn from these passages about how we should view and use Scripture? Honour it as the word of God. Use it in context

3. How can we make the Bible central to church life today? You might find it helpful to answer these questions on verses of chapter eight:

   - To what part of Jerusalem did the people come? into city
   - Why did they choose that place? area big enough

- Who came?
- What did they all do?
- What ability did they all have in common?

4. Many questions arise out of Nehemiah 8 which provide a good opportunity to help us look at our own use of the Bible.

v5, 6	The people praised God who gave them the book. How can we use the Bible to bring us nearer to God in our worship?
v7–9	The Levites explained the Law. Have you found any helps to understanding the Bible particularly good? Which ones? How have you used them?
v10–12	The people were joyful when they understood things from the Law. Have you an experience of Bible reading giving you joy which you'd like to share with the rest of the group? Do so, now. Or have you benefitted in any other way from recent Bible reading?
v13–15	When the study group searched the Law they found a command to obey. How can we best use the Bible as a guide to daily life?
v16–18	The book was read day after day. Do you have a method of daily Bible reading which you follow? What is it? Do you find it easy or difficult to read the Bible regularly? Can you recommend anything that you have found which makes it easier? What?

SESSION SIX

A FRESH START

1–2 On the twenty-fourth day of the same month the people of Israel assembled to fast in order to show sorrow for their sins. They had already separated themselves from all foreigners. They wore sackcloth and

put dust on their heads as signs of
grief. Then they stood and began to
confess the sins that they and their
ancestors had committed. 3 For about
three hours the Law of the LORD their
God was read to them, and for the next
three hours they confessed their sins
and worshipped the LORD their God.

4 There was a platform for the
Levites, and on it stood Jeshua, Bani,
Kadmiel, Shebaniah, Bunni,
Sherebiah, Bani, and Chenani. They
prayed aloud to the LORD their God.

5 The following Levites gave a call to
worship: Jeshua, Kadmiel, Bani,
Hashabneiah, Sherebiah, Hodiah,
Shebaniah, and Pethahiah. They said:

"Stand up and praise the LORD your God;
praise him for ever and ever!
Let everyone praise his glorious name,
although no human praise is great enough."

6 And then the people of Israel
prayed this prayer:

"You, LORD, you alone are LORD;
you made the heavens and the stars of the sky.
You made land and sea and everything in them;
you gave life to all.
The heavenly powers bow down and worship you.
7 You, LORD God, chose Abram
and led him out of Ur in Babylonia;
you changed his name to Abraham.
8 You found that he was faithful to you,
and you made a covenant with him.
You promised to give him the land of the Canaanites,
the land of the Hittites and the Amorites,
the land of the Perizzites, the Jebusites, and the Girgashites,
to be a land where his descendants would live.
You kept your promise, because you are faithful.
9 "You saw how our ancestors suffered in Egypt;
you heard their call for help at the Red Sea.
10 You worked amazing miracles against the king,
against his officials and the people of his land,
because you knew how they oppressed your people.
You won then the fame you still have today.
11 Through the sea you made a path for your people
and led them through on dry ground.
Those who pursued them drowned in deep water,
as a stone sinks in the raging sea.
12 With a cloud you led them in daytime,
and at night you lighted their way with fire.
13 At Mount Sinai you came down from heaven;
you spoke to your people
and gave them good laws and sound teachings.
14 You taught them to keep your Sabbaths holy,
and through your servant Moses you gave them your laws.

15 "When they were hungry, you gave them bread from heaven,
and water from a rock when they were thirsty.
You told them to take control of the land
which you had promised to give them.
16 But our ancestors grew proud and stubborn
and refused to obey your commands.
17 They refused to obey; they forgot all you did;
they forgot the miracles you had performed.
In their pride they chose a leader
to take them back to slavery in Egypt.
But you are a God who forgives;

you are gracious and loving, slow
to be angry.
Your mercy is great; you did not
forsake them.
18 They made an idol in the shape of a
bull-calf
and said it was the god who led
them from Egypt!
How much they insulted you, LORD!
19 But you did not abandon them there
in the desert,
for your mercy is great.
You did not take away the cloud or
the fire
that showed them the path by day
and night.
20 In your goodness you told them
what they should do;
you fed them with manna and
gave them water to drink.
21 Through forty years in the desert
you provided all that they needed;
their clothing never wore out,
and their feet were not swollen
with pain.

22 "You let them conquer nations and
kingdoms,
lands that bordered their own.
They conquered the land of
Heshbon, where Sihon ruled,
and the land of Bashan, where Og
was king.
23 You gave them as many children as
there are stars in the sky,
and let them conquer and live in
the land
that you had promised their
ancestors to give them.
24 They conquered the land of Canaan;
you overcame the people living
there.
You gave your people the power to
do as they pleased
with the people and kings of
Canaan.
25 Your people captured fortified cities,
fertile land, houses full of wealth,
cisterns already dug,
olive-trees, fruit-trees, and
vineyards.
They ate all they wanted and grew
fat;
they enjoyed all the good things
you gave them.

26 "But your people rebelled and
disobeyed you;
they turned their backs on your
Law.
They killed the prophets who
warned them,
who told them to turn back to you.
They insulted you time after time,
27 so you let their enemies conquer
and rule them.
In their trouble they called to you for
help,
and you answered them from
heaven.
In your great mercy you sent them
leaders
who rescued them from their
foes.
28 When peace returned, they sinned
again,
and again you let their enemies
conquer them.
Yet when they repented and asked
you to save them,
in heaven you heard, and time
after time
you rescued them in your great
mercy.
29 You warned them to obey your
teachings,
but in pride they rejected your
laws,
although keeping your Law is the
way to life.
Obstinate and stubborn, they
refused to obey.
30 Year after year you patiently warned
them.
You inspired your prophets to
speak,
but your people were deaf,
so you let them be conquered by
other nations.
31 And yet, because your mercy is
great,
you did not forsake or destroy
them.
You are a gracious and merciful
God!
32 "O God, our God, how great you are!

How terrifying, how powerful!
You faithfully keep your covenant promises.
From the time when Assyrian kings oppressed us,
even till now, how much we have suffered!
Our kings, our leaders, our priests and prophets,
our ancestors, and all our people have suffered!
Remember how much we have suffered!
33 You have done right to punish us;
you have been faithful, even though we have sinned.
34 Our ancestors, our kings, leaders, and priests
have not kept your Law.
They did not listen to your commands and warnings.
35 With your blessing, kings ruled your people
when they lived in the broad, fertile land you gave them;
but they failed to turn from sin and serve you.
36 And now we are slaves in the land that you gave us,
this fertile land which gives us food.
37 What the land produces goes to the kings
that you put over us because we sinned.
They do as they please with us and our cattle,
and we are in deep distress!"

38 Because of all that has happened, we, the people of Israel, hereby make a solemn written agreement, and our leaders, our Levites, and our priests put their seals to it.

Chapter 10

28 We, the people of Israel, the priests, the Levites, the temple guards, the temple musicians, the temple workmen, and all others who in obedience to God's Law have separated themselves from the foreigners living in our land, we, together with our wives and all our children old enough to understand,
29 do hereby join with our leaders in an oath, under penalty of a curse if we break it, that we will live according to God's Law, which God gave through his servant Moses; that we will obey all that the LORD, our Lord, commands us; and that we will keep all his laws and requirements.

Nehemiah 9.1–38; 10.28, 29.

The celebration is over and the time has come for Nehemiah's people to say sorry for the bad things they have done and to re-commit themselves to living as God requires.

Before the group meeting

Repentance 9.1–3

v1 to fast This means to go without food for a while as a religious duty. Its purpose is not self-denial but "self-detachment"—to withdraw from a concern with food in order to devote oneself more to God.

v2 from all foreigners This separation was not meant as an act of arrogance. It was a sign of commitment, and a time to formalize and make public the divorces from foreigners that had already been agreed individually. There is a proper separation of God's people from all others. It is a way in which they can show they belong to God.

Think about:

- How this separation of God's people from others works today. In what ways is it right for members of the Christian community to be involved with those outside it? Are there times when it is not right?

A review 9.7,9,13,15,22, and 30

Verses 6–38 give a summary of the prayers and worship of the community on its special day. The verses you have just read trace the history of the community from Abram's call from God through to its sin and conquest. It might be helpful for you to mark these verses so that you can see at a glance where you are in this passage.
The history of God's people becomes the framework for their prayer. It is also the focal point of their prayers because they have realized that by breaking God's laws they have not realized the blessings available to them.

Think about:

- Times when you have not obeyed God's commandments and have felt as if you have missed out on blessings from God as a result.

The great God 9.6,10,15,24,27, and 30

One thing emerges clearly from the review of history; how great God is. Each verse gives examples of his abilities. Read through the verses again and note down the things that each one tells you God has done!

v6 ______________________________

v10 ______________________________

v15 ______________________________

v24 ____________________

v27 ____________________

v30 ____________________

Compassion 9.17,27,28, and 31

The Hebrew word for compassion appears in three different ways in these verses. It is translated as loving (v17) mercy (v27, 28, and 31) and merciful (v31). In these verses the Lord is described as acting in certain ways as a result of his compassion.

Try to make a list of what he does.

v17 ____________________

v27 ____________________

v28 ____________________

v31 ____________________

Sin 9.10,16,17,26,29,33, and 34

The light of God's compassion and love shines through a great deal of Israel's history. But there is a darker side as well; the darkness of the people's disobedience.

Think about the types of wrongdoing mentioned in these verses and consider whether they are things which we still do today and how we might begin not to do them.

Commitment 9.38; 10.28–29

What was the result of the Israelites realizing God's greatness and compassion in comparison with their own sinfulness?

What should be the result when we come to realize the same things for ourselves?

At the group meeting

1. Think about the verses you have studied since the last session. Is there anything arising from them you want to discuss with the rest of the

group? Make sure everyone has sufficient time to share any ideas, thoughts, or questions they might have.

2. Chapter 9.3 suggests a time division for time spent with God. How do you structure your time alone with God if you have one? Is this a similar sort of division of time?

   Do Nehemiah's people do some things that you do not?

   Do you do some things that they do not?

3. What is sin? Once again, think about the sins mentioned in this passage and your answer to the question about them. Do you think that any of the areas mentioned in the passage are particularly applicable to the church today? If so, which ones? What can we do about them? What do you think are your community's clearest areas of obedience to God's laws?

4. As we have seen, God showed his compassion in many ways throughout Israel's history. Have you an experience of God's goodness and compassion that you can tell the group?

   Are there anybody else's experiences of God's goodness that it would encourage group members to hear about?

5. This passage shows us different aspects of prayer. What can we learn about prayer from it and about the sort of prayers we should pray?

SESSION SEVEN

NO EASY SOLUTION

10 I also learnt that the temple
musicians and other Levites had left
Jerusalem and gone back to their
farms, because the people had not
been giving them enough to live on. 11 I
reprimanded the officials for letting
the Temple be neglected. And I
brought the Levites and musicians
back to the Temple and put them to
work again. 12 Then all the people of
Israel again started bringing to the
temple storerooms their tithes of corn,
wine, and olive-oil. 13 I put the following
men in charge of the storerooms:
Shelemiah, a priest; Zadok, a scholar
of the Law; and Pedaiah, a Levite.

Hanan, the son of Zaccur and grandson
of Mattaniah, was to be their assistant.
I knew I could trust these men to be
honest in distributing the supplies to
their fellow-workers.

14 Remember, my God, all these
things that I have done for your
Temple and its worship.

15 At that time I saw people in
Judah pressing juice from grapes on
the Sabbath. Others were loading
corn, wine, grapes, figs, and other
things on their donkeys and taking
them into Jerusalem; I warned them
not to sell anything on the Sabbath.
[16]Some men from the city of Tyre
were living in Jerusalem, and they
brought fish and all kinds of goods into
the city to sell to our people on the
Sabbath. [17]I reprimanded the Jewish
leaders and said, "Look at the evil
you're doing! You're making the
Sabbath unholy. [18]This is exactly why
God punished your ancestors when he
brought destruction on this city. And
yet you insist on bringing more of God's
anger down on Israel by profaning the
Sabbath."

19 So I gave orders for the city gates
to be shut at the beginning of every
Sabbath, as soon as evening began to
fall, and not to be opened again until
the Sabbath was over. I stationed some
of my men at the gates to make sure
that nothing was brought into the city
on the Sabbath. [20]Once or twice
merchants who sold all kinds of goods
spent Friday night outside the city
walls. [21]I warned them, "It's no use
waiting out there for morning to come.
If you try this again, I'll use force
against you." From then on they did
not come back on the Sabbath. [22]I
ordered the Levites to purify
themselves and to go and guard the
gates to make sure that the Sabbath
was kept holy.

Remember me, O God, for this also,
and spare me because of your great
love.

23 At that time I also discovered that
many of the Jewish men had married
women from Ashdod, Ammon, and
Moab. [24]Half their children spoke the
language of Ashdod or some other
language and didn't know how to
speak our language. [25]I reprimanded
the men, called down curses on them,
beat them, and pulled out their hair.
Then I made them take an oath in God's
name that never again would they or
their children intermarry with
foreigners. [26]I said, "It was foreign
women that made King Solomon sin.
He was a man who was greater than
any of the kings of other nations. God
loved him and made him king over all
Israel, and yet he fell into this sin. [27]Are
we then to follow your example and
disobey our God by marrying foreign
women?"

28 Joiada was the son of Eliashib the
High Priest, but one of Joiada's sons
married the daughter of Sanballat, from
the town of Beth Horon, so I made
Joiada leave Jerusalem.

29 Remember, O God, how those
people defiled both the office of priest
and the covenant you made with the
priests and the Levites.

30 I purified the people from
everything foreign; I prepared
regulations for the priests and the
Levites so that each one would know
his duty; [31]I arranged for the wood
used for burning the offerings to be
brought at the proper times, and for
the people to bring their offerings of
the first corn and the first fruits that
ripened.

Remember all this, O God, and give
me credit for it.

Nehemiah 13.10–31

At the end of the last session the people of Jerusalem had made a solemn agreement before God. Chapter 10 lists the names of the leaders who signed the document. Chapters 11 and 12 tell us more about the city; who was permitted to live there and about the splendid ceremony the day the wall was dedicated (12.27–43). We learn (13.6–7) that Nehemiah had returned to the king, probably honouring the agreement made in 2.6, but he returned to Jerusalem later to find things weren't quite going according to his plans.

Before the group meeting

Giving 13.10–13

The solemn agreement in Chapter 10 mentioned three specific points of commitment to God. The third of these (10.32–39) concerned maintaining the work of the Temple by regular giving. When Nehemiah returned it was clear that the people had not kept their promises. In preparation for the group meeting think about how you decide to give and how regular your contribution is.

The Sabbath ignored 13.15–18

The second commitment in the agreement had been to obey God's law concerning the seventh day and the seventh year (10.31) as well as the rest of the obligatory feasts. (Details of these can be found in Exodus 20.8–11; Leviticus 25.1–7; Exodus 23.14–17, etc.) Upon his return Nehemiah found that these things had slipped and he feared God's anger.

The Sabbath observed 13.19–22

Nehemiah wasn't content simply to reprimand his people and warn them of the consequences of their actions. He was determined to make sure that the Sabbath was observed and used his authority to enforce it.

Think about:

- How you observe the Sabbath.
- If you help others to observe it or not and how you do this.

Separation 13.23–27

The third commitment concerned the separateness and distinctness of the people of God (10.30). Yet again the people were not keeping their promise. Clearly it is one thing to make promises to God and another to keep them.

- Have you ever made a promise to God which you have broken? What was it?
- Have you ever made a promise to a person which you have broken? What was it? What happened?

Laws for everyone 13.28–29

Here we can see that Nehemiah treated everyone alike. Even the High Priest's son was not exempt.

Think about how you treat individuals. Do you think of them as equals no matter who and what they are? Should you? Give examples.

Well done, Nehemiah 13.30–31

Just like the heroes of faith in Hebrews 11 Nehemiah kept his eyes on the future reward (Hebrews 11.26). He sought to run his particular race in such a way as to win the prize (1 Corinthians 9.24).

- In what ways do you run your race so as to win the prize? What does this mean to you?
- Have you ever done anything that you hope God will remember you for doing? What?

At the group meeting

1. For the final time reflect upon the readings during the week. Discuss together:
    - Any problems raised.
    - Any problems solved.
    - Anything that particularly spoke to you.
2. Generosity proves the commitment is real. Would you agree?

Read these verses out in the group and make notes about what they say to you about giving.

Deuteronomy 14.22 ______________________

____

Malachi 3.10 ______________________

____

Mark 12.41–44 ______________________

____

Acts 2.45 ______________________

____

Acts 11.27–29 ______________________

____

Romans 12.8 ______________________

____

2 Corinthians 8.1–2 ______________________

____

2 Corinthians 8.13–14 ______________________

____

Philippians 4.17–18 ______________________

____

Now draw up some guidelines for Christian giving.

3. How do you make Sunday a special day?

Here is another set of verses to read round the group. Write down the thought which comes to you each time.

Exodus 20.8–11 ______________________

____

Exodus 23.12 ______________________

____

Exodus 31.16–17 ______________________

____

Isaiah 56.2,6–7 ______________________

____

Mark 2.27–28 ____________________

____

Mark 3.4 ____________________

____

Colossians 2.16–17 ____________________

____

Now draw up some guidelines that would help people to make Sunday a special day.

4. In the New Testament and the Old (Romans 12.2ff, James 4.4ff) God's people are called to be different. How can we do this without being aloof or arrogant?

   What would be the best distinguishing marks of a Christian in today's world? What would they be in your particular circumstances?

   What is the difference between Christian "separateness" and some other groups who have wished to remain separate with unfortunate consequences?